AF867113

The Asset Manager's Guide to Silver

Roggie Clark

Continue Learning At Our Website: Roggieclarkbooks.com

Continue exploring educational resources, tools, books, workbooks, and learning materials designed to help readers continue building knowledge and practical skills. Visit: www.roggieclarkbooks.com

Inside you'll find:

- Educational worksheets
- Beginner-friendly guides
- Printable activities
- Companion materials for books and courses

A growing library of educational content for readers, collectors, learners, parents, teachers, and lifelong students.

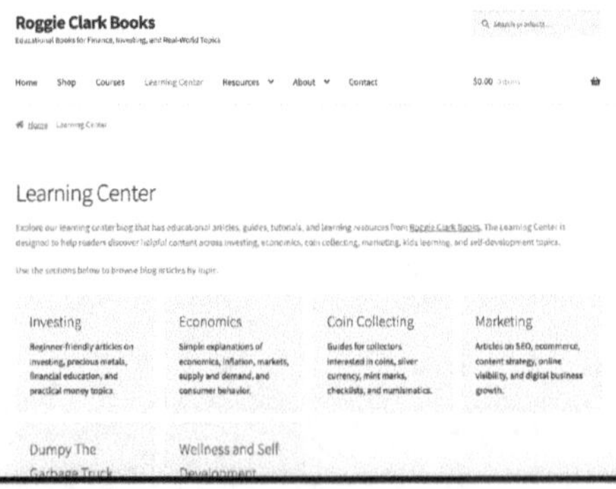

Learn Macro and Micro Economics, With This One Book

Whether you're a student, a professional, or simply someone eager to understand the world around you, this book is your perfect introduction to the fundamentals of micro and macroeconomics.

The Strategic Guide to U.S. Mint Gold and Silver Coin Investing

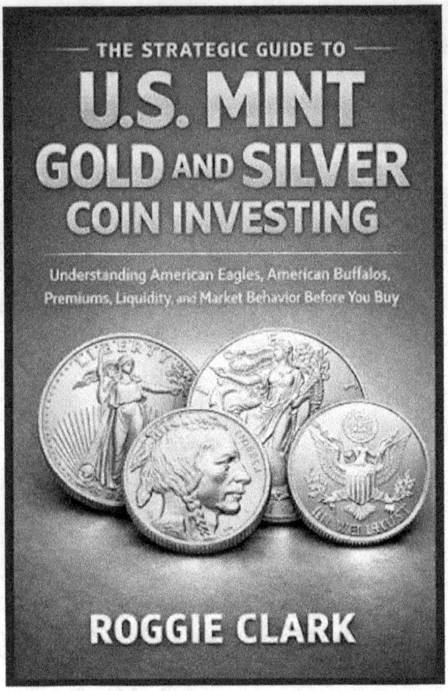

Rather than offering a general introduction to precious metals, this guide examines how American Gold Eagles, American Gold Buffalos, and Silver American Eagles behave in real investor markets.

Copyright

Title: The Asset Manager's Guide to Silver
Author: Roggie Clark

Cover Design: Roggie Clark
Editing: Renee' Clark

Printed in the United States of America

Disclaimer

The views and opinions expressed in this publication are those of the author and do not necessarily reflect the official policies, positions, opinions, or viewpoints of any individual, company, organization, institution, agency, or entity referenced or mentioned within this work.

The author is not necessarily affiliated with, endorsed by, sponsored by, or compensated by any individuals, companies, organizations, brands, institutions, products, or services referenced within this publication unless specifically stated otherwise. Any examples, sample situations, stories, illustrations, or scenarios presented may be fictionalized or simplified for educational purposes. Any resemblance to actual persons, living or dead, businesses, or events is purely coincidental unless otherwise stated.

The information, ideas, strategies, concepts, techniques, opinions, suggestions, and educational materials contained in this publication are provided on an "as is" basis without warranties of any kind, either express or implied. While every effort has been made to provide accurate and current information, neither the author nor the publisher makes any representations or warranties regarding the completeness, accuracy, reliability, suitability, or applicability of the information presented.

This publication is intended solely for educational and informational purposes and should not be interpreted as professional advice of any kind, including but not limited to financial, investment, legal, tax, business, medical, mental health, educational, psychological, or other professional guidance. Readers should conduct their own independent research and consult appropriately qualified professionals before making decisions that may affect their finances, health, business, education, legal matters, personal circumstances, or other important areas of life.

Results, outcomes, and experiences may vary significantly among individuals. Neither the author nor the publisher guarantees any specific outcomes, results, earnings, performance improvements, personal achievements, or benefits resulting from the use of information contained in this publication.

By reading, accessing, or using this publication, you acknowledge and agree that the author and publisher shall not be held liable for any direct, indirect, incidental, consequential, financial, personal, emotional, or other damages, losses, or claims arising from the use, misuse, interpretation, or application of information contained within this publication. You assume full responsibility for any actions, decisions, and outcomes resulting from the use of this material.

Image Credits and Public Domain Notice

All images, illustrations, graphics, photographs, visual references, and related materials included in this publication are believed to be in the public domain, used under applicable licenses or permissions, created by the author or publisher, or obtained from sources that clearly identify them as available for lawful use.

The author and publisher have made a good faith effort to use only visual materials that are lawfully available for use and distribution. Where applicable, images and visual materials may have been resized, cropped, edited, enhanced, stylized, modified, reformatted, or arranged for educational, informational, design, formatting, or presentation purposes.

This publication is intended for educational, informational, and illustrative purposes only. The inclusion of any image, artwork, photograph, visual reference, symbol, historical material, design, or graphic element is not intended to claim ownership over public domain materials or any third-party intellectual property rights that remain with their respective owners.

If you believe any image or visual material included in this publication has been used in error, please contact the author or publisher so the matter may be reviewed and corrected in future editions or releases if necessary.

Any factual information, specifications, historical references, values, descriptions, statistics, or related content accompanying visual materials are provided for general informational purposes only and may change over time. Readers should conduct their own independent research and consult appropriate sources or qualified professionals when making decisions based on information presented in this publication.

This publication is independently produced and is not affiliated with, endorsed by, sponsored by, or associated with any company, organization, government agency, institution, trademark holder, or third party unless specifically stated otherwise.

Table of Contents

Introduction

Silver occupies an unusual position within the investment landscape. It is a precious metal with a long history as money and a store of value, but it is also an industrial material used throughout the modern economy. This combination gives silver characteristics that can make it behave differently from stocks, bonds, gold, and many other commodities. For asset managers and financial advisors, understanding these differences is important when determining whether silver deserves a place within a client's portfolio. The objective is not simply to decide whether silver is a good or bad investment. The more useful question is what role silver may serve, which clients may benefit from exposure, and how that exposure can be incorporated into a broader investment strategy.

Why Silver Deserves Consideration in Modern Portfolios

Modern portfolios provide investors with access to an enormous range of assets. Stocks and bonds continue to form the foundation of many investment strategies, but investors can also allocate capital to real estate, commodities, private markets, precious metals, and other alternative investments. Within this expanding investment universe, **silver** represents an asset that deserves careful evaluation because its performance can be influenced by forces that differ from those affecting traditional securities.

Silver does not generate earnings, dividends, or interest. An investor who owns silver is therefore not purchasing a claim on the future cash flows of a company or receiving contractual payments from a borrower. Instead, silver's market value is determined by the interaction of supply, demand, investment activity, industrial consumption, economic expectations, currency conditions, and broader market sentiment.

These characteristics create both opportunities and limitations. Silver can experience periods of substantial appreciation, but it can also experience significant volatility. Investors should not assume that its status as a precious metal automatically makes it a stable asset. In fact, understanding silver requires recognizing that its price can respond rapidly to changing expectations in both financial and industrial markets.

From a portfolio perspective, this makes silver particularly interesting. An asset does not necessarily need to outperform every other investment to provide value within a diversified portfolio. Its usefulness may instead come from how it behaves in relation to other holdings.

This is where **correlation** becomes important. Portfolio diversification is not achieved simply by accumulating a large number of investments.

Effective diversification involves combining assets whose return drivers are not identical. If every investment responds to the same economic forces in approximately the same way, owning numerous positions may provide less diversification than expected.

Silver may introduce exposure to a combination of monetary, commodity, industrial, and investor-demand factors. These characteristics can give it a different return profile from conventional stocks and bonds. However, correlations change over time, and silver should never be assumed to provide diversification under every market condition.

Asset managers therefore need to evaluate silver within the complete portfolio. The question is not whether silver can rise in value. Almost any investable asset can experience periods of strong performance. The more important question is whether an allocation supports a client's broader objectives while remaining consistent with the client's tolerance for volatility, liquidity requirements, investment horizon, and financial circumstances.

Silver's Dual Role as a Precious Metal and Industrial Commodity

One of the most important concepts for understanding silver is its **dual role**. Silver belongs to the precious-metals market alongside gold, but a meaningful portion of demand for silver is also connected to industrial applications.

As a precious metal, silver has historically been associated with money, wealth storage, bullion ownership, and investment demand. Investors can purchase physical silver in forms such as coins, rounds, and bars. Financial markets also provide other methods for obtaining silver exposure, allowing the metal to function as an investable asset within modern portfolios.

Investment demand can be influenced by concerns about inflation, currencies, monetary policy, financial instability, and general market uncertainty. When investors become more interested in precious metals, silver can attract capital alongside gold.

Yet silver is not simply a smaller or less expensive version of gold.

Silver also possesses physical properties that make it useful in numerous industrial applications. Its electrical and thermal characteristics contribute to its use across electronics, electrical components, energy technologies, manufacturing, and other areas of the global economy. Consequently, changes in industrial activity can influence demand for the metal.

This industrial component introduces an important distinction for asset managers. Economic conditions that might increase investor interest in precious metals can simultaneously influence industrial demand in a different direction.

For example, economic uncertainty could increase investor interest in precious metals while a slowdown in manufacturing reduces demand from certain industrial users. Conversely, strong economic expansion and technological investment may support industrial consumption even when demand for defensive investments is less pronounced.

Silver therefore sits at the intersection of multiple market forces.

This helps explain why silver can sometimes display considerable price volatility. Its market must continuously balance investment demand, industrial consumption, mining production, recycling, inventories, and expectations about future economic conditions.

The distinction also matters when comparing silver with gold. Both are precious metals, and their prices can sometimes respond to similar macroeconomic developments. However, their underlying demand structures are not identical. Asset managers should therefore avoid assuming that an investment thesis for gold automatically applies to silver.

Understanding this difference will be important throughout this book. Silver should be evaluated on its own characteristics rather than simply being treated as an alternative way to obtain precious-metals exposure.

How Asset Managers Should Approach Silver

Asset managers should approach silver in much the same way they would approach any other potential portfolio allocation: begin with the client's objectives and determine whether the investment serves a clearly defined purpose.

This requires moving beyond predictions about where silver prices might go next.

Market forecasts can be useful inputs into investment decisions, but **professional portfolio management** requires a broader framework. Advisors must consider risk tolerance, investment horizon, liquidity needs, existing portfolio exposures, tax considerations, implementation costs, and the client's overall financial circumstances.

A client primarily interested in long-term capital growth may evaluate silver differently from a client concerned about diversification or wealth preservation. A retiree drawing income from a portfolio may have different requirements from a younger investor accumulating assets. High-net-worth families and institutional investors may introduce additional considerations involving liquidity, custody, investment policy, and portfolio governance.

The purpose of the allocation should therefore come first.

An asset manager might evaluate silver as a potential diversification asset, a precious-metals allocation, a commodity exposure, or a tactical position based on a particular economic outlook. Each objective can lead to a different approach regarding position size, investment vehicle, monitoring, and rebalancing.

Implementation matters as well. Physical silver provides direct ownership of the metal, but it introduces considerations involving storage, insurance, transaction costs, and liquidity. Exchange-traded products may provide greater operational convenience, while silver-related equities introduce company-specific and equity-market risks in addition to exposure to the underlying metal.

These investments should not automatically be treated as interchangeable.

Asset managers must also communicate silver's limitations clearly. Silver can decline in value. It can remain below previous highs for extended periods. It does not produce income simply by being held, and its volatility may be inappropriate for certain clients or allocation sizes.

The goal is therefore not to convince every client to own silver.

The goal is to understand the asset well enough to determine when silver may support a client's investment objectives and when it may not. When an allocation is appropriate, the asset manager should also be able to explain why silver is being included, what role it is expected to serve, how exposure will be obtained, what risks accompany the position, and under what circumstances the allocation will be reviewed.

That disciplined approach separates portfolio management from speculation.

Last Thoughts

Silver presents asset managers with a distinctive portfolio question because it cannot be understood exclusively as a precious metal or exclusively as an industrial commodity. Its investment characteristics emerge from the interaction of both roles. That combination can create diversification opportunities while also introducing volatility and economic sensitivity that must be carefully considered.

For investment professionals, the purpose of studying silver is not to develop a universal recommendation. Different clients have different objectives, portfolios, time horizons, and tolerances for risk. A silver allocation that makes sense for one investor may be unnecessary or inappropriate for another.

Throughout this book, we will examine silver from that professional perspective. We will begin by understanding silver as an investment asset before examining portfolio construction, implementation methods, client allocation and risk management, different economic environments, and finally the development of a disciplined professional allocation framework. The objective is to give asset managers the knowledge needed to evaluate silver based on **portfolio purpose, client suitability, and disciplined investment management**, rather than headlines, enthusiasm, or short-term price movements.

Chapter 1: Understanding Silver as an Investment Asset

Silver has occupied an important place in commerce, monetary systems, and personal wealth for thousands of years. Although modern financial markets provide investors with access to countless securities and alternative assets, silver continues to attract attention from individual investors, financial advisors, asset managers, and institutions. Its appeal comes from a combination of scarcity, global recognition, investment demand, and industrial usefulness. For asset managers, however, understanding silver requires looking beyond its reputation as a precious metal. Before determining whether silver belongs in a client portfolio, investment professionals should understand how its role has evolved, what influences its market value, and how its characteristics differ from gold and traditional financial assets.

Silver's History as Money, Wealth, and an Investment

Silver's relationship with wealth stretches back thousands of years. Ancient civilizations valued the metal for its appearance, durability, scarcity, and usefulness in trade. Over time, silver became deeply connected to monetary systems, with silver coins circulating as recognized forms of money across numerous societies.

This monetary history helped establish silver as a **store of value**. People could hold silver outside of ordinary commercial transactions and preserve a portion of their wealth in a tangible asset. The metal could also be transported, divided into standardized quantities, and exchanged, characteristics that contributed to its usefulness in early monetary systems.

As economies became more sophisticated, governments increasingly standardized coinage. Silver coins became part of national and international commerce, with governments controlling their weight, purity, and denomination. The connection between silver and money became so established that the metal remained an important monetary asset for centuries.

Eventually, monetary systems changed.

Modern economies gradually moved toward fiat currencies and financial systems in which circulating money was no longer dependent on precious-metal content. Silver's direct monetary role diminished, particularly as everyday transactions shifted toward paper currency, bank deposits, electronic payments, and other forms of money.

Yet the disappearance of silver from everyday monetary circulation did not eliminate its investment appeal.

Instead, silver increasingly transitioned from circulating money into an **investable precious metal**. Investors could continue holding silver as bullion even though they were no longer using silver coins to purchase ordinary goods and services.

This distinction is important for asset managers. The historical use of silver as money contributes to its modern investment identity, but contemporary silver markets operate very differently from the monetary systems of previous centuries. Today's investor purchases silver within sophisticated global commodity and financial markets rather than relying on the metal as an everyday medium of exchange.

Physical ownership remains one of the most recognizable ways investors participate in the silver market. Bullion coins, rounds, and bars allow investors to own specific quantities of the metal directly. Modern financial markets have also expanded the range of available silver investment vehicles, making exposure possible without necessarily possessing physical bullion.

Silver's industrial importance has simultaneously grown alongside its investment market.

This creates a significant difference between silver's historical and modern roles. An investor centuries ago might have viewed silver primarily as money or stored wealth. A modern asset manager must consider those traditional precious-metal characteristics alongside demand created by industrial activity and technological development.

Silver's long history therefore provides context, but history alone should not determine whether the metal belongs in a portfolio.

For investment professionals, the relevant question is how those historical characteristics interact with the realities of today's silver market. Silver's monetary legacy helps explain why investors continue to recognize it as a financial asset, while its modern industrial applications introduce additional forces that influence supply, demand, and price.

What Drives the Silver Market

Understanding silver requires understanding that its price does not respond to one single variable. The **silver market** reflects interactions among investors, industrial users, miners, refiners, bullion dealers, financial institutions, manufacturers, and other participants.

One major influence is investment demand.

Investors may become interested in silver for several reasons. Some want exposure to precious metals. Others may be concerned about inflation, currency purchasing power, financial instability, or geopolitical uncertainty. Still others may purchase silver because they believe its market price offers an attractive investment opportunity.

Changes in investor sentiment can therefore affect demand for physical bullion and financial products connected to silver.

Industrial demand introduces another important influence. Because silver is used in a variety of industrial and technological applications, changes in manufacturing activity and technological development can affect the amount of silver required by businesses.

This means that asset managers must consider both financial-market conditions and developments within the broader economy.

Supply matters as well.

New silver enters the market primarily through mining, while recycled silver can return existing metal to available supply. Changes in mine production, production costs, recycling activity, and the economics of extracting silver can influence the balance between supply and demand.

Silver production also has an unusual characteristic. Not all silver is produced from mines whose primary purpose is extracting silver. Some silver enters the market as a byproduct of mining other metals. Consequently, silver supply may sometimes be influenced by economic decisions occurring elsewhere in the mining industry.

This can make the supply side of the market more complicated than simply assuming that higher silver prices will immediately result in substantially greater silver production.

Currency movements are another consideration. Silver is traded internationally, and changes in major currencies can influence investor demand and the relative cost of the metal for buyers in different markets.

Interest rates can also affect the investment environment surrounding silver. Because physical silver does not generate interest or other contractual income, the attractiveness of holding a non-yielding asset can change as returns available from cash and fixed-income investments change.

However, these relationships should not be treated as mechanical rules. Silver does not automatically rise whenever interest rates decline, nor does it necessarily fall whenever rates increase. Financial markets incorporate expectations about inflation, economic growth, monetary policy, currencies, and future conditions simultaneously.

Investor positioning can add another layer of volatility.

Silver trades in physical markets as well as through financial instruments, meaning short-term market movements may reflect changing expectations and trading activity in addition to developments in underlying physical supply and demand.

For asset managers, this complexity is important.

A recommendation based on only one silver narrative can overlook other forces affecting the market. For example, an advisor who views silver exclusively through the lens of inflation may miss changes in industrial demand. Someone focused only on industrial consumption may underestimate the influence of precious-metals investment flows.

Silver should therefore be evaluated as a market influenced by several interconnected drivers rather than a metal whose price can be explained by one economic indicator.

How Silver Differs from Gold and Traditional Assets

Silver and gold are frequently discussed together. Both are precious metals, both have long histories as stores of wealth, and both can be purchased as physical bullion or accessed through financial markets.

Yet treating the two metals as interchangeable can create problems for portfolio construction.

One of the most important differences is the significance of **industrial demand** within the silver market. Gold has industrial applications as well, but silver's industrial role is particularly important to understanding its market behavior. This can make silver more sensitive to developments in manufacturing, technology, and broader economic activity.

Silver can therefore respond simultaneously to some of the forces affecting precious metals and some of the forces affecting industrial commodities.

That combination can contribute to greater price fluctuations.

Gold is frequently viewed by investors primarily through the lenses of wealth preservation, monetary conditions, reserve holdings, and financial uncertainty. Silver can attract investors for similar reasons, but its industrial exposure introduces another source of demand that may strengthen or weaken depending on economic conditions.

This distinction becomes particularly important during economic slowdowns. A difficult economic environment could increase interest in precious metals while simultaneously weakening certain forms of industrial demand. Silver may therefore experience competing forces that do not affect gold in precisely the same manner.

Silver also differs substantially from stocks.

A stock represents ownership in a business. Shareholders may benefit from corporate earnings, business expansion, dividends, and increases in the market value of the company. Silver represents no ownership interest in an operating enterprise and produces no corporate earnings.

Bonds are different as well. A traditional bond represents a contractual lending relationship in which an issuer generally agrees to make specified payments. Silver provides no comparable contractual cash flow.

This **lack of income generation** has important implications for asset managers.

When evaluating stocks or bonds, professionals can examine expected earnings, cash flows, interest payments, creditworthiness, and other financial characteristics. Silver must be evaluated differently because its investment return is primarily dependent on changes in market value, minus the costs associated with obtaining and maintaining exposure.

Physical silver can introduce additional considerations involving premiums, spreads, storage, insurance, and security. Financial silver products may introduce their own expenses, structural considerations, and forms of risk. These differences will become particularly important when we examine implementation methods later in the book.

Silver also differs from many traditional assets in how its value is established.

There is no company whose future profits can be projected to estimate silver's intrinsic value using a conventional equity valuation model. There is no maturity date at which silver promises to return principal. Instead, its price emerges from global supply and demand across investment, industrial, and physical markets.

These differences do not inherently make silver better or worse than traditional investments. They simply mean it serves a different potential function.

For an asset manager, that distinction is critical. Silver should not be expected to perform the job of an income-producing bond or a growth-oriented equity investment. Its potential value within a portfolio must instead be considered in relation to its particular return drivers, risks, diversification characteristics, and the client's reason for owning it.

Last Thoughts

Silver's evolution from monetary metal to modern investment and industrial asset helps explain why it remains relevant within financial markets. Its historical association with money and stored wealth continues to influence investor perceptions, while industrial demand has introduced an important economic dimension to the modern silver market. These characteristics distinguish silver not only from traditional stocks and bonds, but also from gold.

For asset managers, recognizing these differences is the foundation for making thoughtful allocation decisions. Silver should not be recommended simply because it is a precious metal, nor should its investment case be based entirely on expectations about industrial growth. Its potential role comes from the interaction of several market forces and from how those characteristics affect the portfolio as a whole.

Understanding the asset itself is only the beginning. The next chapter will examine **Silver and Portfolio Construction**, including silver's relationship with stocks, bonds, gold, and commodities, its potential diversification characteristics, and the differences between strategic and tactical silver allocations.

Chapter 2: Silver and Portfolio Construction

Understanding silver as an investment asset provides the foundation for a more important question: how might it function within a diversified client portfolio? Asset managers rarely evaluate an investment solely on its standalone return potential. They must also consider how an asset interacts with existing holdings, whether it introduces meaningful diversification, and what purpose the allocation is intended to serve. Silver presents an interesting portfolio construction challenge because its precious-metal characteristics can connect it to gold, while its industrial demand can create exposure to economic forces associated with commodities and global growth. Determining whether those characteristics are useful requires examining silver within the context of the complete portfolio rather than treating it as an isolated investment.

Silver's Relationship with Stocks, Bonds, Gold, and Commodities

Portfolio construction involves combining assets with different sources of return and risk. Stocks, bonds, precious metals, commodities, cash, and alternative investments can each respond differently to changing economic and financial conditions. Understanding these relationships helps asset managers determine whether adding a particular investment meaningfully changes a portfolio.

Silver's relationship with stocks is particularly interesting because the two assets can be influenced by some of the same economic developments while responding differently to others.

Stocks represent ownership in businesses, meaning their long-term performance is influenced by corporate profitability, economic growth, productivity, interest rates, and investor expectations. Silver does not represent ownership in a business. However, its industrial applications mean that economic activity can still influence demand for the metal.

During periods of strong manufacturing activity, expanding technology investment, or rising industrial consumption, demand for silver may receive support from the broader economy. This can occasionally cause silver and equities to respond positively to similar economic developments.

That relationship can change when financial uncertainty becomes more important.

Investors sometimes increase their interest in precious metals during periods of concern about currencies, inflation, financial instability, or geopolitical events. Under those circumstances, silver's precious-metal characteristics may become more influential than its connection to industrial activity.

Silver's relationship with bonds is different.

Traditional bonds can provide income and may serve as a source of stability within certain portfolios. Their performance is affected by interest rates, inflation expectations, credit conditions, maturity, and issuer-specific risks. Silver produces no contractual income and has no maturity date, meaning its role within a portfolio is fundamentally different.

Changes in interest rates can nevertheless influence both markets. When yields available from interest-bearing assets become more attractive, investors may evaluate the opportunity cost of holding non-yielding assets such as silver differently. When inflation expectations or concerns about purchasing power increase, precious metals may receive greater attention.

These relationships are not fixed, however. Asset managers should be cautious about assuming that silver will automatically move in the opposite direction of bonds or equities.

Silver's relationship with gold is generally more intuitive.

Both metals participate in the precious-metals market and can attract investors seeking tangible assets, alternative stores of wealth, or exposure outside traditional securities. They can therefore respond to some of the same changes in monetary expectations, investor sentiment, currencies, and financial uncertainty.

But their behavior can diverge.

Gold's investment identity is more heavily associated with wealth preservation, monetary conditions, and reserve assets. Silver's substantial industrial role introduces economic sensitivities that can influence its price independently of gold.

This distinction means that owning silver and owning gold are not necessarily equivalent portfolio decisions.

Silver also belongs within the broader **commodity landscape**. Like other commodities, its market is affected by physical supply, production economics, inventories, and demand from end users. Yet silver's precious-metal status differentiates it from commodities whose demand is driven primarily by consumption.

For asset managers, these overlapping relationships are part of what makes silver distinctive. It can display characteristics associated with precious metals, industrial commodities, and alternative investments without fitting perfectly into any one category.

The appropriate portfolio question is therefore not simply, "What does silver behave like?" It is, "How does silver interact with the particular assets this client already owns?"

Diversification and Correlation Considerations

Diversification is one of the fundamental principles of portfolio management. Its purpose is not merely to increase the number of investments in a portfolio. The objective is to reduce excessive dependence on any single source of risk or return.

This makes the relationship between assets important.

Two investments that consistently respond to the same economic forces in similar ways may provide less diversification than their different names suggest. Conversely, an asset that behaves differently under certain conditions may contribute useful balance even if its standalone volatility is relatively high.

Silver's potential diversification benefits arise partly from the variety of forces that influence its market.

Stocks may be heavily affected by corporate earnings and economic expectations. Bonds may respond strongly to interest rates, inflation expectations, and credit conditions. Silver can be influenced by industrial consumption, precious-metal investment demand, currency movements, physical supply, mining activity, and investor sentiment.

Because those drivers are not identical, silver may sometimes behave differently from traditional portfolio holdings.

However, asset managers should not confuse diversification with guaranteed protection.

Silver can decline at the same time as stocks. It can also decline during periods of economic uncertainty. In severe market disruptions, investors may sell multiple types of assets simultaneously as they seek liquidity or reduce risk.

The effectiveness of diversification therefore depends partly on **correlation**, which describes how the returns of different assets move in relation to one another.

Correlation is not permanent.

Relationships between asset classes can strengthen, weaken, or reverse as economic conditions change. Silver may display one relationship with equities during an industrial expansion and another during a period dominated by monetary uncertainty. Its relationship with gold can also vary depending on which forces are driving precious-metals markets.

This is why historical relationships should be interpreted carefully. Past correlations can help asset managers understand how assets have interacted, but they do not guarantee that the same relationships will persist.

Position size also matters.

Adding a very small amount of an asset may have little effect on overall portfolio behavior. An excessively large allocation, on the other hand, can allow that asset's volatility to dominate the portfolio and potentially undermine the diversification objective.

The goal is not to maximize exposure to every diversifying asset. It is to determine whether the allocation contributes meaningfully to the intended portfolio structure without introducing disproportionate risk.

Asset managers should also consider what kind of diversification they are seeking.

A client heavily concentrated in equities may want exposure to assets with different market drivers. Another client may already own substantial commodities or precious metals, meaning additional silver could increase concentration rather than improve diversification.

This reinforces an important principle: diversification must be evaluated at the **portfolio level**.

Silver does not possess a universal diversification value independent of everything else an investor owns. Its usefulness depends on the existing portfolio, the size of the proposed allocation, the investment vehicle being used, and the client's objectives.

A well-diversified portfolio is ultimately a collection of intentional exposures. Silver may contribute to that structure, but only when its role is clearly understood.

Strategic Versus Tactical Silver Allocations

Once an asset manager determines that silver may serve a useful portfolio function, another decision becomes necessary: whether the exposure should be **strategic or tactical**.

A strategic allocation is generally designed to remain part of the portfolio over a longer investment horizon. The manager identifies a reason for owning the asset, establishes an appropriate target allocation or range, and maintains exposure as part of the portfolio's broader structure.

Under this approach, silver might be included because the manager believes its different market drivers contribute to diversification or because precious metals have an ongoing role within the client's investment policy.

The emphasis is not on predicting short-term price movements.

Instead, the allocation is maintained because silver is expected to serve a particular portfolio function across different market environments. Positions can be monitored and periodically rebalanced, but the underlying reason for owning silver remains relatively stable.

A **tactical allocation** operates differently.

Tactical investing involves adjusting portfolio exposure in response to a particular market view, valuation assessment, economic expectation, or perceived opportunity. An asset manager might temporarily increase silver exposure because of expectations involving precious-metals demand, industrial activity, monetary conditions, or another market development.

The potential advantage of tactical management is flexibility. Managers can adjust exposure as their outlook changes rather than maintaining a constant allocation.

The difficulty is that tactical decisions depend much more heavily on timing.

An asset manager can correctly identify a long-term trend while still entering the position too early, exiting too soon, or misjudging how financial markets will respond. Short-term silver prices can be volatile, and multiple market forces may operate simultaneously.

Tactical allocations can therefore introduce additional decision-making risk.

There is also a behavioral consideration. Without a clearly defined process, tactical investing can become a justification for reacting to headlines. A sharp increase in silver prices may encourage investors to buy after substantial appreciation, while a decline may cause them to abandon an allocation when sentiment is weakest.

Professional management requires distinguishing deliberate tactical positioning from emotional market chasing.

Some portfolios may combine strategic and tactical approaches. A manager might maintain a core silver allocation while allowing exposure to move within predetermined limits when conditions justify an adjustment.

Whatever approach is selected, the rationale should be established before the investment is made.

Asset managers should understand why silver is being purchased, what would justify changing the position, how large the allocation may become, and what conditions would cause the original investment thesis to be reconsidered.

This creates discipline.

Strategic and tactical silver allocations are not inherently superior to one another. They simply represent different approaches to portfolio management. The appropriate choice depends on the client's objectives, the manager's investment process, and the intended role of silver within the portfolio.

Last Thoughts

Silver can occupy an unusual position within portfolio construction because its market behavior reflects characteristics of both precious metals and industrial commodities. Those characteristics may allow silver to interact differently with stocks, bonds, gold, and other commodities, potentially giving asset managers another source of portfolio diversification.

However, diversification should never be assumed simply because an asset is different. Correlations can change, silver can experience substantial volatility, and an inappropriate allocation size can introduce more risk than diversification benefit. Asset managers must evaluate silver in relation to the client's complete portfolio rather than judging the metal solely by its historical performance.

The purpose of the allocation also matters. Strategic exposure can provide a long-term place for silver within an established investment framework, while tactical exposure allows managers to respond to specific market opportunities or expectations. In either case, the decision should begin with a clearly defined portfolio objective.

The next chapter will move from portfolio construction to **Silver Investment Vehicles and Implementation**, examining physical silver bullion, coins and bars, silver funds and exchange-traded products, and silver mining stocks and other forms of indirect exposure.

Chapter 3: Silver Investment Vehicles and Implementation

Once an asset manager determines that silver may serve an appropriate role within a client portfolio, the next decision involves implementation. Investors do not have to obtain silver exposure in the same way, and the vehicle selected can significantly affect liquidity, costs, operational requirements, and risk. Direct ownership of physical bullion provides a very different experience from holding a silver fund or investing in a mining company. For asset managers, the objective is not to identify one universally superior method. It is to understand how the available approaches differ and select an implementation method that aligns with the client's objectives and the intended purpose of the silver allocation.

Physical Silver Bullion, Coins, and Bars

Physical ownership is perhaps the most recognizable way to invest in silver. Investors can purchase **physical bullion** in several forms, including government-issued bullion coins, privately produced rounds, and bars of various sizes.

The primary characteristic of physical silver is direct ownership. Rather than holding shares in a financial product or ownership in a company, the investor owns the metal itself.

This simplicity can be attractive to certain clients.

Some investors specifically want tangible precious-metal ownership. They may prefer having an asset that exists outside of a traditional stock or bond investment and does not depend on the operating performance of a particular company.

Physical ownership, however, introduces practical considerations that asset managers must evaluate.

One of the first is the difference between the market price of silver and the price an investor actually pays for a physical product. Bullion dealers generally sell silver above the underlying market value of its metal content. This additional cost is commonly known as a **premium**.

Premiums can vary according to the type of product, market conditions, supply availability, dealer pricing, and investor demand. Smaller products may sometimes carry higher premiums relative to the amount of silver purchased, while larger bars can provide a more efficient way to acquire substantial quantities.

Selling physical silver can also involve a difference between the price at which a dealer sells the product and the amount the dealer is willing to pay to purchase it. Asset managers should therefore consider transaction costs in addition to movements in the underlying silver price.

Storage represents another important consideration.

An investor who possesses physical silver must determine where it will be kept. Smaller holdings may be stored personally, while larger allocations may require professional storage or custodial arrangements. Security, insurance, accessibility, and cost can all become relevant.

Silver also presents a practical storage consideration because of its value relative to its physical size and weight. A substantial dollar allocation to silver can require considerably more physical storage capacity than an equivalent dollar allocation to a higher-value precious metal such as gold.

Liquidity should also be evaluated.

Silver bullion is widely traded, but selling physical metal requires finding an appropriate buyer, agreeing on a price, and completing the transaction. This process differs from selling a publicly traded security through a brokerage account.

Product selection matters as well.

Government-issued bullion coins may be familiar and easily recognizable to many market participants. Privately produced rounds and bars can provide other options for obtaining physical silver exposure. Asset managers considering direct ownership should focus on the investment characteristics of the product rather than allowing collectible appeal to become confused with the purpose of the portfolio allocation.

Collectible and rare coins can carry values influenced by scarcity, condition, historical significance, and collector demand. Those characteristics introduce risks and valuation considerations that differ from straightforward bullion investing.

For a portfolio designed primarily to track silver's market value, investment-grade bullion products may provide a more direct relationship with the underlying metal than collectible items whose prices depend on additional factors.

Physical silver can therefore be appropriate for clients who value direct ownership and understand the operational requirements involved. It may be less suitable for portfolios that require rapid trading, simple rebalancing, or minimal storage responsibilities.

Silver Funds and Exchange-Traded Products

Financial markets provide investors with ways to obtain silver exposure without personally storing bullion. Among the most accessible are **silver funds and exchange-traded products** designed to provide exposure to the silver market.

These vehicles can simplify implementation considerably.

Instead of arranging for the purchase, transportation, storage, and eventual sale of physical bullion, investors can generally purchase eligible exchange-traded silver products through investment accounts in much the same way they purchase other publicly traded securities.

For asset managers overseeing multiple client portfolios, this convenience can be particularly important.

Exchange-traded exposure can make it easier to establish positions of specific sizes, adjust allocations, execute portfolio-wide changes, and rebalance holdings when necessary. Market pricing also provides a readily observable value for the position during trading hours.

Liquidity can be another advantage.

A sufficiently liquid exchange-traded product may allow an asset manager to increase or decrease silver exposure more efficiently than purchasing or selling physical bullion. This can be useful for clients whose portfolios require regular rebalancing or whose liquidity needs could change.

However, owning shares in a silver-related financial product is not identical to personally possessing silver.

The structure of the product matters.

Asset managers should understand what the investment actually holds, how it seeks to provide silver exposure, what expenses it charges, how shares are created and redeemed, and what risks arise from its particular structure.

Some products may hold physical silver, while other approaches can obtain commodity exposure through different financial arrangements. These distinctions can affect how closely the investment behaves relative to movements in the underlying silver market.

Tracking differences are another consideration. Fees, operating expenses, trading conditions, and product structure can cause an investment's return to differ from movements in the silver price over time.

This may be relatively modest in some products, but even small recurring expenses can affect long-term results.

Asset managers should also examine trading characteristics. Bid-ask spreads, market liquidity, fund size, and trading volume can influence the cost and efficiency of establishing or exiting a position.

The appropriate product therefore depends on more than simply finding an investment with "silver" in its name.

Professionals should understand the underlying exposure before recommending a vehicle to clients.

For many portfolios, the operational simplicity of exchange-traded exposure can be attractive. It can allow silver to be managed within the same investment infrastructure used for other portfolio holdings, making allocation monitoring and rebalancing more straightforward.

Yet convenience should not replace due diligence. The investment vehicle should support the reason silver was added to the portfolio in the first place.

Silver Mining Stocks and Other Indirect Exposure

Another way investors can participate in the silver market is through companies involved in producing the metal. **Silver mining stocks** can provide exposure to businesses whose financial performance may benefit when silver-market conditions are favorable.

However, owning a mining company is fundamentally different from owning silver.

A share of mining stock represents ownership in a business. Its value can therefore be affected by silver prices, but it is also influenced by the company's costs, production levels, reserves, management decisions, financing, geographic exposure, regulatory environment, and overall financial condition.

This creates both opportunity and additional risk.

When silver prices rise while production costs remain relatively stable, a mining company's profitability may increase substantially. Because the company's revenues can increase faster than certain costs, mining equities may sometimes provide amplified exposure to favorable silver-market conditions.

The opposite can also occur.

Declining silver prices can place pressure on revenue and profitability. Operational problems, rising labor or energy costs, equipment failures, permitting difficulties, political developments, or disappointing production can hurt a mining company even when the underlying silver market is relatively strong.

Mining equities also remain equities.

During broad stock-market declines, silver mining shares may experience pressures associated with the equity market in addition to developments affecting silver itself. Investors seeking silver primarily because they want an asset with characteristics different from stocks should therefore recognize that mining companies may not fulfill the same portfolio function as physical bullion or a product designed to track silver more directly.

Another complication is that mining businesses do not always produce only one metal. Some companies may generate revenue from silver alongside gold, copper, lead, zinc, or other resources. As a result, the company's performance may reflect several commodity markets rather than silver alone.

Investors can also obtain indirect exposure through diversified mining funds rather than selecting individual companies. Such funds can spread company-specific risk across multiple holdings, although they remain exposed to risks associated with the mining industry and equity markets.

Other businesses connected to precious-metal production can provide additional forms of indirect exposure. Their economics and contractual arrangements can differ substantially from those of traditional mining operators.

Asset managers should therefore distinguish between **metal exposure and business exposure**.

If the objective is to obtain relatively direct exposure to movements in silver prices, physical bullion or appropriately structured silver products may more closely match that purpose. If the objective includes exposure to businesses that could potentially benefit from favorable conditions in the silver industry, mining-related investments may be considered.

Neither approach should automatically substitute for the other.

Implementation should always follow portfolio purpose. The vehicle an asset manager selects determines not only how the client participates in the silver market, but also what additional risks, costs, and operational considerations enter the portfolio.

Last Thoughts

Investors have several ways to obtain exposure to silver, but those methods should not be treated as interchangeable. Physical bullion provides direct ownership while introducing premiums, storage, security, and transaction considerations. Silver funds and exchange-traded products can simplify portfolio implementation and rebalancing, but their structures, expenses, liquidity, and tracking characteristics require careful evaluation. Mining stocks and other indirect investments introduce business and equity-market risks that extend beyond movements in the underlying metal.

For asset managers, implementation decisions should follow the reason silver is being included in the portfolio. A client seeking direct precious-metal ownership may require a different solution from a client prioritizing liquidity and efficient rebalancing. Likewise, an investor willing to accept greater company-specific and equity risk may view mining-related investments differently from someone seeking more direct silver exposure.

Selecting the investment vehicle is therefore only one part of the allocation process. The next chapter, **Client Allocation Strategies and Risk Management**, will examine how asset managers can determine appropriate silver allocations, match exposure to client objectives, and manage volatility, concentration, and broader portfolio risk.

Chapter 4: Client Allocation Strategies and Risk Management

Determining how to obtain silver exposure is only part of the asset manager's responsibility. The next challenge is deciding how much exposure may be appropriate, which clients may benefit from it, and how the risks associated with silver should be managed within the broader portfolio. There is no single silver allocation that is suitable for every investor. Differences in financial objectives, existing holdings, investment horizons, liquidity requirements, and tolerance for price fluctuations can lead to very different conclusions. For this reason, professional silver recommendations should begin with the client rather than with a prediction about the metal's future price.

Determining Appropriate Silver Allocations

One of the most difficult questions surrounding silver is also one of the most straightforward: how much should a client own?

There is no universal percentage that answers this question.

An appropriate allocation depends first on the purpose silver is expected to serve. If silver is being introduced as a relatively small source of diversification, the position may look very different from an allocation intended to provide broader precious-metals or commodity exposure.

The client's existing portfolio also matters.

An investor whose wealth is concentrated heavily in equities may have a different reason for considering silver than an investor who already maintains substantial allocations to gold, commodities, mining companies, or other alternative assets. Adding silver to the second portfolio could increase an existing concentration rather than create meaningful diversification.

Asset managers should therefore examine the client's total exposure rather than viewing the proposed silver position independently.

The type of silver investment being used must also be considered.

A particular percentage allocated to physical bullion does not necessarily create the same portfolio characteristics as an identical percentage invested in silver mining stocks. As discussed in the previous chapter, mining companies introduce operational and equity-market risks that direct ownership of the metal does not.

Allocation decisions should therefore consider both the size of the position and the nature of the exposure.

Silver's price behavior deserves particular attention. Because silver can experience substantial movements over relatively short periods, even an initially modest position can become a larger portion of the portfolio after significant appreciation. The opposite can happen after a major decline.

This makes **allocation ranges** useful within a professional investment framework.

Rather than viewing a target as an exact percentage that must remain unchanged at all times, an asset manager can establish acceptable boundaries around the position. This provides room for ordinary market fluctuations while identifying circumstances in which the allocation should be reviewed or rebalanced.

Position size should also reflect the client's ability to tolerate volatility.

An investor may express enthusiasm for silver during a period of rising prices without fully appreciating how they would respond to a substantial decline. Asset managers should evaluate whether the proposed allocation could create losses large enough to cause the client to abandon the strategy at an unfavorable time.

The investment horizon is another consideration.

Clients with longer horizons may have more time to tolerate periods of weakness, while clients with near-term spending requirements may place greater importance on stability and liquidity. Silver should not be used to satisfy financial obligations that require predictable values at specific dates.

Liquidity needs can influence both allocation size and implementation. A client who may need ready access to capital should be evaluated differently from an investor who can maintain long-term exposure without relying on the silver allocation for near-term expenses.

Ultimately, determining an appropriate silver allocation requires balancing potential portfolio benefits against the risks created by the position.

The objective is not to maximize silver exposure. It is to determine whether an allocation of an appropriate size can serve its intended function without becoming disproportionately important to the client's financial outcome.

Matching Silver Exposure to Client Objectives

Different clients can have very different reasons for considering silver. Understanding those reasons is essential because the same investment can serve different functions depending on the portfolio in which it is placed.

For a client primarily focused on long-term growth, silver may occupy a supporting rather than central position.

Growth-oriented investors generally rely heavily on productive assets capable of generating earnings, cash flows, or economic value over time. Because silver does not generate these forms of income, a large allocation could reduce the portion of the portfolio devoted to assets designed primarily for long-term compounding.

That does not necessarily exclude silver from a growth portfolio. It simply means the reason for including it should be clearly distinguished from the role played by growth-oriented investments.

Clients focused on **wealth preservation** may approach silver differently.

These investors may be interested in holding assets outside conventional securities or maintaining some exposure to precious metals. Silver's history, tangible nature, and global market may make it relevant to that objective.

However, wealth preservation should not be confused with price stability. Silver can experience meaningful declines, and clients should understand that owning a precious metal does not guarantee preservation of principal over every investment period.

Retirees present another set of considerations.

Many retirees need portfolios capable of supporting withdrawals while maintaining sufficient liquidity and controlling overall risk. Because silver does not inherently produce income, it generally cannot fulfill the same role as an income-producing investment.

A retiree considering silver therefore needs to understand how the allocation fits alongside assets being used to generate cash flow and fund spending needs.

High-net-worth clients and family wealth structures may approach silver from a broader perspective. They may already hold multiple asset classes and seek exposure to assets with different economic drivers. Some may also value direct ownership of physical precious metals as part of a larger wealth strategy.

Institutional clients can introduce still different requirements. Their allocations may need to comply with investment policies, liquidity requirements, governance procedures, custody standards, and established risk limits.

Asset managers should also consider the client's expectations.

A client who believes silver will automatically protect a portfolio during every recession or inflationary period may be approaching the investment with unrealistic assumptions. Recommending an allocation without addressing those expectations can create problems later if silver behaves differently from what the client anticipated.

This makes **client communication** an important part of the allocation process.

The advisor should be able to explain what silver is expected to contribute to the portfolio, what it is not expected to accomplish, how the position will be implemented, and what risks could cause it to perform poorly.

The conversation should also address the client's comfort with the investment itself.

Some clients may appreciate tangible bullion but dislike the responsibilities associated with storage and security. Others may prefer exchange-traded exposure because it integrates easily with an existing portfolio. Still others may be comfortable with the additional risks associated with mining equities.

Matching silver exposure to client objectives therefore involves more than choosing an allocation percentage.

It requires matching the purpose, investment vehicle, position size, and expectations surrounding the investment to the individual client.

Managing Volatility, Concentration, and Portfolio Risk

Silver introduces several risks that asset managers should consider before and after an allocation is established.

Among the most visible is **volatility**.

Silver prices can move considerably over relatively short periods. These movements may be driven by changes in investment sentiment, industrial expectations, currencies, monetary conditions, commodity markets, or broader financial developments.

Volatility is not automatically a reason to exclude an investment from a portfolio. Many assets capable of contributing to long-term portfolio objectives experience periods of substantial price movement.

The important consideration is whether the amount of volatility introduced is appropriate for the client.

Position sizing provides one method of controlling that exposure. A volatile asset held at a modest allocation may have a limited effect on the complete portfolio, while the same asset held at a very large allocation can become a dominant source of portfolio risk.

This leads to **concentration risk**.

Silver can attract considerable investor attention during periods of rapidly rising prices or heightened economic uncertainty. Clients may become tempted to increase exposure because recent performance has been strong or because they have developed strong convictions about future economic conditions.

Asset managers should be careful about allowing enthusiasm for a single investment thesis to overwhelm broader diversification principles.

Concentration can also develop unintentionally.

A client may own physical silver, a silver exchange-traded product, mining stocks, and a broader precious-metals fund without recognizing that several positions respond to overlapping market forces. Looking at each holding independently can therefore understate the client's total exposure.

Professional risk management requires identifying these connections.

Asset managers should also consider **liquidity risk**. Different silver vehicles offer different levels of convenience when positions need to be reduced or converted to cash. Physical holdings can involve dealer transactions and transportation or custody considerations, while financial products have their own market-liquidity characteristics.

Implementation costs represent another source of risk to investment outcomes. Premiums, spreads, storage expenses, fund fees, and other costs can reduce the return the client ultimately receives from silver exposure.

Ongoing monitoring is therefore necessary.

As silver prices change, the position may drift away from its intended allocation. A substantial increase can cause silver to represent a much larger share of the portfolio than originally planned, while a significant decline can reduce the allocation below its strategic target.

Periodic **rebalancing** can restore the intended portfolio structure.

Rebalancing does not require predicting whether silver is about to rise or fall. Its purpose is to maintain the risk exposures established through the client's investment strategy.

Asset managers should also periodically revisit the original reason for owning silver.

A change in the client's financial circumstances, liquidity requirements, investment horizon, or objectives may alter the suitability of an existing position even if nothing fundamental has changed within the silver market.

Risk management therefore extends beyond monitoring the metal's price.

The asset manager must monitor the relationship between silver and the client's broader financial plan. The relevant question is not simply whether the investment is profitable. It is whether silver continues to perform the portfolio function for which it was originally selected.

Last Thoughts

Silver allocation decisions should begin with client objectives rather than market enthusiasm or predictions about future prices. Appropriate exposure depends on the role silver is intended to serve, the client's existing portfolio, investment horizon, liquidity requirements, tolerance for volatility, and the particular vehicle being used to obtain exposure.

These considerations become especially important because silver can experience substantial price movements. Position sizing, allocation ranges, diversification, monitoring, and rebalancing can help prevent a supporting portfolio asset from becoming an unintended source of excessive concentration.

Professional risk management also requires recognizing that silver's risks extend beyond price movements. Liquidity, implementation costs, overlapping exposures, and changes in client circumstances can all affect whether an allocation remains appropriate.

With these client-level considerations established, the next chapter will examine **Silver Across Economic and Market Environments**, including silver during inflation, interest rate and currency changes, the influence of industrial demand during economic growth and recessions, and silver's behavior during periods of financial and geopolitical uncertainty.

Chapter 5: Silver Across Economic and Market Environments

Silver does not operate independently from the broader economy. Its price can be influenced by monetary conditions, currencies, investor demand, industrial activity, and expectations about economic growth. This makes understanding different market environments particularly important for asset managers. Silver's dual role means that the forces affecting it can sometimes reinforce one another and, at other times, move in opposing directions. Rather than assuming that silver will behave predictably whenever inflation rises, interest rates change, or markets become unstable, investment professionals should understand the different channels through which economic conditions can affect the metal.

Silver During Inflation, Interest Rate, and Currency Changes

Inflation is frequently mentioned as one of the reasons investors consider precious metals. When the purchasing power of money becomes a concern, investors may look for assets whose value is not directly tied to a particular currency.

Silver can become part of that conversation.

Because silver is a globally traded physical asset with limited supply, some investors view it as a potential **inflation hedge**. Rising prices throughout the economy can increase interest in precious metals, particularly when investors become concerned about the long-term purchasing power of cash.

However, asset managers should avoid presenting silver as an automatic hedge against inflation.

Inflation can arise for different reasons, and financial markets respond not only to current inflation but also to expectations about future monetary policy, economic growth, currencies, and interest rates. Silver may perform strongly during some inflationary periods while behaving differently during others.

The response of central banks can be particularly important.

When inflation rises substantially, monetary authorities may increase interest rates in an effort to slow economic activity and control price pressures. Higher rates can make interest-bearing assets more attractive relative to assets that do not generate income.

This creates an important consideration for silver.

Because silver itself does not produce interest, changes in the return available from cash and fixed-income investments can affect investor preferences. If investors can obtain attractive returns from relatively conservative interest-bearing assets, the opportunity cost of holding silver may increase.

Asset managers should pay particular attention to **real interest rates**, which consider the relationship between nominal interest rates and inflation.

An environment in which interest rates are high but inflation is even higher can create different incentives from an environment in which interest rates substantially exceed inflation. Investors are ultimately concerned not only with the nominal return they receive, but also with how much purchasing power that return preserves.

Currency movements introduce another layer.

Silver is traded globally, and changes in major currencies can affect both investment demand and the effective price paid by participants in different countries. Movements in the U.S. dollar are often particularly relevant because international commodity markets commonly reference dollar-denominated prices.

A strengthening dollar can make dollar-priced commodities more expensive for some international buyers, while a weakening dollar can have the opposite effect. Currency expectations can also influence investors who view precious metals as alternatives to holding monetary assets.

Again, these relationships are not mechanical.

Silver does not necessarily rise every time a currency weakens or decline every time interest rates increase. Several forces may be operating simultaneously, including industrial demand, investor positioning, supply conditions, and expectations about future economic activity.

For asset managers, the more useful approach is to understand how inflation, rates, and currencies contribute to the broader environment surrounding silver.

These variables should be considered together rather than used as isolated signals for making allocation decisions.

Industrial Demand, Economic Growth, and Recessions

Silver's industrial applications distinguish it from an asset whose value is driven primarily by investment demand. This means that changes in the **economic cycle** can have important implications for the silver market.

During periods of economic expansion, manufacturing activity can increase as businesses produce more goods, invest in equipment, expand infrastructure, and respond to growing consumer and commercial demand.

Industries that use silver can contribute to demand during these periods.

Technological development can also influence consumption. Silver's physical characteristics make it useful in a variety of electrical and industrial applications, meaning changes in technology and manufacturing can affect how much silver the global economy requires.

This industrial exposure can provide a source of demand that differs from traditional precious-metals investment.

However, the same relationship can create challenges during economic slowdowns.

A recession can reduce manufacturing activity, business investment, and demand for certain industrial products. If industries consuming silver reduce production, industrial demand for the metal may weaken.

This creates an interesting tension.

Economic weakness may encourage some investors to become more interested in precious metals because of concerns about financial markets or monetary conditions. At the same time, weakening industrial activity may place pressure on another important source of silver demand.

The resulting market behavior depends partly on which force becomes dominant.

This is one reason asset managers should be cautious about assuming that silver will behave exactly like gold during recessions. Silver's industrial exposure can cause the two metals to respond differently even when both are receiving attention from precious-metals investors.

Economic recoveries can create another set of conditions.

As manufacturing and investment activity improve, industrial demand may strengthen. If investor interest in precious metals remains elevated at the same time, silver could potentially receive support from both sides of its demand structure.

The opposite combination is also possible. Industrial activity could improve while investors reduce precious-metals exposure as confidence in traditional financial markets strengthens.

Supply conditions further complicate the relationship.

Mining companies cannot necessarily adjust production immediately when economic conditions change. Developing mines, expanding production, obtaining permits, and investing in infrastructure can require substantial time and capital. Because some silver is produced alongside other metals, production decisions may also reflect conditions in markets beyond silver itself.

Asset managers should therefore avoid reducing silver's industrial story to a simple assumption that economic growth is always positive and recession is always negative.

The relationship is more nuanced.

Economic activity influences one important source of silver demand, while financial conditions and investor behavior influence another. Understanding the interaction between these forces provides a more complete picture of how silver may behave across different stages of the economic cycle.

Silver During Financial and Geopolitical Uncertainty

Periods of financial instability can cause investors to reconsider the risks within their portfolios. Banking stress, severe market declines, sovereign debt concerns, geopolitical conflicts, and other unexpected developments can increase demand for assets perceived as being different from conventional financial securities.

Precious metals often receive attention during these periods.

Silver may benefit from increased **safe-haven demand** when investors become concerned about financial stability, currencies, or the broader economic outlook. Its long history as a precious metal can contribute to this perception.

However, silver should not be described as a guaranteed safe haven.

Periods of severe financial stress can create unusual market behavior. Investors may sell assets that they would normally prefer to hold because they need cash, want to reduce leverage, or are attempting to meet other financial obligations.

This can create a **liquidity event** in which many different assets decline simultaneously.

Silver can be affected by these conditions.

Its industrial role may also influence its response. If financial instability is expected to produce a severe economic slowdown, concerns about future industrial demand can exist alongside increased investor interest in precious metals.

Geopolitical uncertainty introduces similar complexity.

Military conflicts, trade disruptions, political instability, sanctions, and tensions between major economies can alter expectations about inflation, currencies, energy costs, supply chains, and economic growth.

Silver can be influenced indirectly through all of these channels.

Some investors may increase precious-metals exposure because they want assets that are not directly dependent on the financial performance of individual companies or governments. Others may respond by moving toward cash or highly liquid securities.

Asset managers should therefore avoid assuming that geopolitical headlines alone provide a reliable signal for increasing silver exposure.

This is particularly important when communicating with clients.

Periods of uncertainty can encourage emotional investment decisions. Clients may become interested in silver after dramatic news events because they believe a major economic disruption is imminent. Others may want to make substantial portfolio changes based on fear.

Professional portfolio management requires maintaining perspective.

If silver was already included as part of a long-term allocation strategy, periods of uncertainty do not necessarily require dramatic changes. The portfolio should continue to be evaluated according to its established objectives, allocation ranges, and risk parameters.

This is one reason **portfolio resilience** can be a more useful objective than attempting to predict every crisis.

A resilient portfolio is designed to remain aligned with client objectives across a variety of possible environments rather than depending entirely on one economic forecast. Silver may contribute to that framework for some investors because its return drivers differ from those of certain traditional assets.

But silver itself is not a complete risk-management strategy.

Its usefulness depends on how it interacts with the other holdings in the portfolio and whether the size and structure of the allocation remain appropriate for the client.

Last Thoughts

Silver's behavior across different economic environments reflects the same characteristic that makes the metal distinctive: it responds to both investment and industrial forces. Inflation, interest rates, currencies, economic growth, recessions, financial instability, and geopolitical uncertainty can all influence silver, but they do not operate independently or produce predictable outcomes every time.

For asset managers, understanding these environments should therefore support portfolio analysis rather than encourage market timing based on individual economic indicators. Silver may benefit from certain conditions while facing competing pressures from others, particularly when its precious-metal and industrial roles pull the market in different directions.

The objective is not to identify the economic environment in which silver is guaranteed to perform well. No such environment exists. Instead, investment professionals should understand the conditions that can influence silver and evaluate whether its characteristics support the client's broader portfolio objectives across multiple possible outcomes.

The next chapter, **Building a Professional Silver Allocation Framework**, will bring these concepts together by examining how asset managers can establish silver's purpose within the portfolio, monitor and rebalance positions, and avoid common mistakes when managing silver allocations.

Chapter 6: Building a Professional Silver Allocation Framework

Understanding silver's characteristics, investment vehicles, portfolio relationships, and behavior across different economic environments provides asset managers with the information needed to evaluate the metal. The final step is turning that knowledge into a repeatable investment process. Professional portfolio management requires more than identifying an attractive asset or developing a market outlook. It requires establishing why an investment belongs in the portfolio, defining how it will be managed, and creating guidelines for reviewing decisions over time. A professional silver allocation framework can help ensure that silver remains connected to client objectives rather than becoming a position driven by changing headlines, short-term price movements, or investor emotion.

Establishing Silver's Purpose Within the Portfolio

Every portfolio allocation should have a reason for existing.

Before adding silver, an asset manager should be able to explain what the position is intended to accomplish and how it supports the client's broader investment strategy. Without this foundation, it becomes difficult to determine an appropriate allocation, select an investment vehicle, or evaluate whether the position is fulfilling its intended role.

This begins with establishing an **investment rationale**.

For one client, silver may be included as part of a broader precious-metals allocation. Another portfolio may use it to introduce exposure to an asset influenced by both investment and industrial demand. A different client may hold silver as part of a diversified allocation to commodities or alternative assets.

These objectives are related, but they are not identical.

The reason for owning silver should influence how the position is constructed. A long-term strategic allocation may require different guidelines from a tactical position established because of a particular market outlook.

The investment vehicle should also correspond with the objective.

If direct ownership is important to the client, physical bullion may be appropriate. If efficient portfolio management, liquidity, and straightforward rebalancing are priorities, an exchange-traded approach may be more practical. If the objective involves gaining exposure to businesses that could benefit from favorable silver-market conditions, mining-related investments may be considered.

Once the purpose and implementation method have been identified, the asset manager can establish a **target allocation**.

The target should reflect the client's objectives, existing portfolio, tolerance for price fluctuations, liquidity requirements, and investment horizon. Because silver can experience substantial volatility, the size of the position should also be considered in relation to the amount of overall portfolio risk it could contribute.

A target does not necessarily need to function as a rigid percentage.

Asset managers may establish an acceptable range around the desired allocation. This allows normal market movements to occur without requiring constant portfolio adjustments while still establishing boundaries that can trigger a review.

Documentation can strengthen this process.

An investment policy or internal portfolio guideline can identify why silver is being held, the acceptable allocation range, permitted investment vehicles, monitoring requirements, and circumstances that could justify changing the position.

This creates accountability.

When silver prices rise rapidly, the manager can return to the original rationale rather than automatically increasing exposure because recent performance has been strong. When prices decline, the same framework can help determine whether the investment thesis has actually changed or whether the position is simply experiencing expected volatility.

Client understanding is equally important.

A professional framework should not exist only within the asset manager's investment process. Clients should understand why silver has been included and what they should reasonably expect from the allocation.

This does not require predicting a particular return.

Instead, the advisor should communicate the intended portfolio function, important risks, expected investment horizon, and circumstances under which the allocation may be adjusted.

Establishing purpose before implementation gives every later decision a reference point. The asset manager is no longer asking whether silver happens to look attractive today. The more relevant question becomes whether the allocation continues to serve the purpose for which it was originally established.

Monitoring, Rebalancing, and Reviewing Silver Positions

Adding silver to a portfolio is not the end of the investment process. Once exposure has been established, the position should be incorporated into the same ongoing oversight applied to other portfolio holdings.

Monitoring begins with allocation size.

Changes in silver prices can cause the position to move above or below its intended range. A period of strong performance may increase silver's percentage of the portfolio even if the asset manager makes no additional purchases.

This can gradually change the portfolio's risk profile.

If a position originally intended to serve as a supporting allocation becomes substantially larger, the client may become more exposed to silver's volatility than the investment strategy originally intended.

Declining prices can create the opposite situation. Silver may fall below its target allocation and become too small to provide the exposure originally sought.

This is where rebalancing becomes useful.

Asset managers can establish **rebalancing guidelines** that determine when portfolio adjustments should be considered. These guidelines can reduce the temptation to make decisions solely because of recent price movements.

One approach is calendar-based rebalancing.

Under this method, the portfolio is reviewed at predetermined intervals. Depending on the broader investment process, reviews might occur quarterly, semiannually, annually, or according to another established schedule.

Another approach is threshold-based rebalancing.

Instead of adjusting positions according to the calendar, the manager reviews the allocation when it moves outside an established range. This allows ordinary fluctuations to occur while identifying larger deviations that may require action.

Some asset managers may combine both approaches.

The portfolio can be reviewed periodically while also establishing thresholds that trigger additional evaluation between scheduled reviews.

However, monitoring should extend beyond the allocation percentage.

The asset manager should periodically evaluate whether the investment vehicle continues to serve its intended purpose. Expenses can change, liquidity conditions can evolve, and operational considerations may make another implementation method more appropriate.

For physical holdings, storage arrangements, insurance, security, and transaction considerations may need periodic review.

For exchange-traded exposure, asset managers may consider liquidity, expenses, structure, and whether the product continues to provide the desired form of silver exposure.

Mining-related investments require additional monitoring because company-specific circumstances can change independently of silver prices.

Client circumstances can change as well.

A client who originally had a long investment horizon may eventually require greater liquidity. Retirement, major purchases, changes in income, estate-planning needs, or changes in risk tolerance can alter the role an existing silver allocation should play.

This makes **portfolio review** broader than simply asking whether silver has increased or decreased in value.

The manager should ask whether the original reason for owning silver remains valid, whether the position remains appropriately sized, whether the implementation method remains suitable, and whether the allocation still aligns with the client's financial circumstances.

Performance should also be evaluated within the context of the original objective.

If silver was included primarily as a diversifying asset, judging the allocation solely against equity-market returns could create misleading conclusions. An asset does not necessarily need to outperform the strongest portfolio holding to fulfill its intended role.

The appropriate evaluation depends on why the asset was purchased.

Consistent monitoring allows asset managers to distinguish between an investment that is temporarily performing poorly and an allocation that no longer serves its intended portfolio function.

Common Silver Allocation Mistakes Asset Managers Should Avoid

A professional framework becomes particularly valuable when markets become emotional. Silver can experience periods of intense investor interest, rapid price appreciation, pessimism, and significant volatility. These conditions can encourage decisions that conflict with disciplined portfolio management.

One common mistake is recommending silver without defining its purpose.

If the only explanation for owning the metal is an expectation that its price will increase, the position can quickly become dependent on market predictions. When those predictions fail to materialize, neither the manager nor the client has a broader framework for determining whether the investment should remain in the portfolio.

Another mistake is **performance chasing**.

Strong silver returns can attract attention from clients who previously had little interest in the metal. Recent appreciation may create a sense that an opportunity is being missed, encouraging investors to increase exposure after substantial gains have already occurred.

Asset managers should distinguish between a legitimate change in the investment case and enthusiasm created by recent performance.

Fear can produce similar behavior in the opposite direction.

Economic uncertainty, inflation concerns, geopolitical events, or dramatic financial headlines can lead clients to view precious metals as guaranteed protection against an anticipated crisis. This can create pressure to establish disproportionately large positions.

Silver should not become a substitute for comprehensive portfolio construction.

Another mistake is failing to account for overlapping exposures.

A client might own physical bullion, silver funds, precious-metals funds, mining companies, and broader commodity investments. Looking at these positions individually may make each allocation appear modest, while the combined exposure could represent a meaningful concentration in related market risks.

Asset managers should evaluate these positions collectively.

Confusing silver with silver mining companies is another potential problem.

As discussed earlier, mining equities represent ownership in businesses. Their performance can be influenced by silver prices, but also by operating costs, management decisions, financing, political conditions, production results, and broader equity-market movements.

A mining stock should therefore not automatically be used as a substitute for direct silver exposure.

Ignoring costs can also weaken an allocation strategy.

Physical bullion can involve premiums, spreads, storage, and insurance. Financial products can charge recurring expenses. Trading activity can create additional transaction costs. These expenses may appear relatively small individually, but they can accumulate over long holding periods.

Another mistake is failing to establish an exit or review process.

Without predetermined guidelines, investors can become uncertain about what to do after substantial gains or losses. A rapidly appreciating silver position may be allowed to grow far beyond its intended size, while a declining position may be sold simply because the investor becomes uncomfortable.

A structured framework replaces these reactions with predefined criteria.

Finally, asset managers should avoid allowing personal convictions about silver to replace **client suitability**.

An advisor may have a strong view about inflation, currencies, industrial demand, or the future price of precious metals. Those views can contribute to investment analysis, but they should not override the client's objectives, financial circumstances, or tolerance for risk.

The responsibility of the asset manager is not to prove a particular market thesis correct.

It is to construct and manage portfolios that remain aligned with the clients they are designed to serve.

Last Thoughts

A professional silver allocation framework transforms silver from an isolated investment idea into a defined component of the portfolio-management process. Establishing the purpose of the position, selecting an appropriate implementation method, setting allocation parameters, and documenting the investment rationale can provide the discipline necessary to manage silver across changing market environments.

That discipline must continue after the investment is made. Monitoring, rebalancing, and periodic portfolio reviews help ensure that silver does not become too large, too small, or disconnected from the objective it was originally intended to serve. Just as importantly, a structured process can help asset managers avoid performance chasing, excessive concentration, overlapping exposures, and emotionally driven decisions.

Silver does not require a completely different philosophy of asset management. It requires the same principles that support thoughtful investment decisions elsewhere: clear objectives, appropriate position sizing, disciplined implementation, ongoing oversight, and a consistent focus on client suitability.

When those principles remain at the center of the process, asset managers can evaluate silver for what it actually is: one potential component within a much larger portfolio, whose value ultimately depends not only on its individual performance, but on how effectively it contributes to the client's broader investment strategy.

Last Thoughts

Silver occupies a distinctive position within modern investment markets. It carries the historical identity of a precious metal while also serving as an important industrial commodity. That combination gives silver characteristics that can differ from stocks, bonds, gold, and other alternative investments. Throughout this book, we have examined those characteristics not to argue that every client should own silver, but to help asset managers determine when silver may serve a legitimate purpose within a professionally constructed portfolio.

For investment professionals, the most important consideration is not whether silver prices are expected to rise next month or next year. Markets are uncertain, and even well-supported forecasts can prove incorrect. A more durable approach begins by identifying the role an investment is expected to serve and determining whether its risks and characteristics align with the client's broader financial objectives.

Silver may provide certain investors with exposure to precious metals, commodities, industrial demand, or assets influenced by market forces that differ from those affecting traditional securities. At the same time, silver introduces meaningful risks. Its price can be volatile, it does not inherently generate income, and its behavior can change as investment demand, industrial activity, monetary conditions, currencies, and economic expectations evolve.

These characteristics reinforce the importance of viewing silver within the complete portfolio.

An allocation that appears reasonable in isolation may become unnecessary when a client already possesses substantial precious-metals or commodity exposure. Similarly, a position that begins as a modest portfolio component can become an unintended concentration after significant price appreciation. Understanding existing exposures, position sizes, and the relationships among holdings remains essential.

Implementation also matters.

Physical bullion, exchange-traded products, mining equities, and other forms of silver exposure can produce substantially different investment experiences. The appropriate vehicle depends on what the client is attempting to accomplish, along with considerations involving liquidity, costs, custody, operational requirements, and tolerance for additional risks.

This is why recommending silver requires more than understanding the metal itself.

Asset managers must understand the client.

A younger investor focused primarily on long-term growth may evaluate silver differently from a retiree managing withdrawals. A high-net-worth investor seeking broader diversification may have different requirements from an institutional portfolio operating under formal investment policies. There is no single allocation or implementation method capable of addressing every circumstance.

Professional management therefore depends on establishing a clear rationale before making the investment.

Once silver enters the portfolio, that rationale provides the foundation for future decisions. Allocation ranges can be established, positions can be monitored, and adjustments can be made through a disciplined review and rebalancing process rather than reactions to headlines or short-term market movements.

Silver's dual identity makes this discipline particularly valuable. At different times, its price may be influenced more heavily by precious-metals investment demand, industrial consumption, economic expectations, monetary conditions, or combinations of these forces. Asset managers should expect those relationships to evolve rather than assuming silver will behave predictably in every inflationary period, recession, financial crisis, or economic expansion.

Ultimately, the purpose of a silver allocation should not be to predict every market environment correctly.

It should be to support the client's broader investment objectives.

Successful asset management is rarely about discovering one asset capable of solving every portfolio challenge. It is about combining investments with different characteristics in a deliberate way, understanding the risks each introduces, and maintaining a process that remains aligned with the investor over time.

Silver can be considered within that process without being treated as either an essential holding or an asset that should automatically be avoided. Its suitability depends on the portfolio, the client, the implementation method, and the reason for owning it.

For asset managers and financial advisors, that is ultimately the most useful way to think about silver: not as a prediction, a trend, or a universal recommendation, but as a potential portfolio tool whose value must be evaluated through **client objectives, disciplined portfolio construction, thoughtful risk management, and professional judgment**.

About the Author

Roggie "Raj" Clark is an entrepreneur and a 10-year marketing professional with a proven track record in e-commerce and digital business growth. Having built and managed successful online stores with thousands of sales and consulted for numerous marketing clients, Roggie has mastered the intricacies of online marketing, branding, and consumer behavior. He has also written several popular books on digital marketing, SEO (search engine optimization), and programming (HTML, CSS, and JavaScript).

As a former marketing manager at a fintech company—a role he secured through his own marketing and financial expertise—Roggie gained firsthand experience in financial strategy and wealth-building. This journey inspired him to share insights with amateur investors, helping them save money, make smarter financial decisions, and build long-term wealth. Raj currently lives in Maryland with his sister and niece.

www.ingramcontent.com/pod-product-compliance
Lightning Source LLC
LaVergne TN
LVHW050827061126
851857LV00012B/1010